Gwendolyn MacEwen was b̶̶̶̶̶̶̶̶̶̶̶̶̶̶̶̶̶̶̶̶̶̶̶̶̶̶̶̶̶ ̶ ̶.
At the age of sixteen her poetry̶ ̶ ̶ ̶ ̶ ̶ ̶ ̶ ̶ ̶in *The Canadian Forum* and she bravely left scho̶ ̶ ̶ two years later to pursue her writing career. Two pamphlets of poetry appeared in 1961 and many collections followed. She twice received the Governor General's Award for Poetry, for *The Shadow-Maker* in 1967, and posthumously for *Afterworlds* (1987). She also wrote plays, including translations, poetry, short stories and two novels. In November 1987 she died of a suspected heart attack.

Selected titles by Gwendolyn MacEwen

Poetry

The Drunken Clock
Selah
The Rising Fire
The Breakfast for Barbarians
The Shadow-Maker
The Armies of the Moon
Magic Animals
The Fire-Eaters
The T.E. Lawrence Poems
Earthlight
Afterworlds

Novels

Julian the Magician
King of Egypt, King of Dreams

Short Fiction

Noman
Noman's Land

The Poetry of Gwendolyn MacEwen

Selected and introduced
by Margaret Atwood

A *Virago* Book

Published by Virago Press 1996

Copyright © The Estate of Gwendolyn MacEwen 1993
Introduction copyright © Margaret Atwood 1996

The poems included are also published in *The Poetry of Gwendolyn MacEwen* (two volumes) edited by Margaret Atwood and Barry Callaghan, published by Exile Editions Limited, Canada 1993

The moral right of the author has been asserted

All rights reserved. No part of this publication may be reproduced, stored in a retrieval system, or transmitted in any form or by any means, without the prior permission in writing of the publisher, nor be otherwise circulated in any form of binding or cover other than that in which it is published and without a similar condition including this condition being imposed on the subsequent purchaser.

A CIP catalogue record for this book is available
from the British Library

ISBN 1 86049 073 5

Typeset by M Rules
Printed and bound in Great Britain by Clays Ltd, St Ives plc

Virago
A Division of
Little, Brown and Company (UK)
Brettenham House
Lancaster Place
London WC2E 7EN

Contents

II.

III.

From *The Shadow-Maker* and *The Armies of the Moon*, 1966–72

IV.

From *The T.E. Lawrence Poems*, 1982

V.

From *Afterworlds*, 1987

ACKNOWLEDGEMENTS

Poems from Section I have been previously published by Contact Press and Ryerson Press; poems in Section II by The Canadian Broadcasting Corporation and McClelland and Stewart; Section III by Macmillan; Section IV by Mosaic Press; and Section V by McClelland and Stewart.

Special thanks go to Rosemary Sulllivan and Barry Callaghan.

Introduction

*For we are great statements in our days
And on the basis of that we can expect small audiences.*

Gwendolyn MacEwen was the most remarkable of her generation of Canadian poets – those who began publishing in the late 1950s to the mid 1960s, and who included among them Leonard Cohen, Michael Ondaatje, John Newlove, Pat Lane and George Bowering. I realise, looking back, that she was also the only woman poet of my own age that I knew personally during those years. She died, unexpectedly and far too young, in 1987, from a suspected heart attack brought on by overuse of alcohol. She was forty-five.

Her childhood – so long a mystery to those of us who knew her – has now been well researched by Rosemary Sullivan in her biography of MacEwen, *The Shadow-Maker*. Her mother was English, from a poor working-class London family; she suffered from mental disturbances as an adolescent. The Scotsman who married her was ignorant of this, but discovered it soon after the young couple had emigrated to Canada. Gwendolyn was born in September 1941, in Toronto. She was the second of two children, and due to her mother's frightening violence and frequent hospitalisations and her father's growing despair and eventual alcoholism, she was brought up largely by an aunt.

Despite this stressful childhood, the conviction that she would be a poet came to her as a saving grace in early adolescence, when she changed her name – the family had called her 'Wendy' – to be ready for it. At the same time she was also mastering the violin and teaching herself Hebrew, which was the first of many languages, including French, Greek and Arabic, that she would later learn. She began publishing poetry in the well-respected journal *The Canadian Forum* when she was sixteen, and at the age of eighteen – although warned against such a rash step by more practical heads – left high school to pursue her vocation, determined to make a living by her writing.

The late 1950s was not the best time for such a move, especially if you were a woman. In the world of conventional North American popular culture, Doris Day and Betty Crocker ruled supreme, and Mom-and-Dad domesticity was the norm. Rebellion was male-only: Marlon Brando and his *Wild Ones* motorbike gang; or rock 'n' roll and jazz; or, in poetry, the Beat Generation, in which women could participate only as compliant helpmeets and payers of the rent. 'Artist' meant male painter; any woman rash enough to take brush in hand was regarded as a dabbler. In fact, women artists of any kind in that still heavily Freudian era were assumed to have adjustment problems. *Man Does, Woman Is*, as Robert Graves so dauntingly put it; and if women insisted on doing, rather than being, they were likely to end up with their heads in the oven, depressive suicides like Sylvia Plath.

So much for gender; then there was location. To be a woman poet was hard enough, but to be one *in Toronto*? At that time Montreal was the cultural heartland of Canada, for both English-speaking and French-speaking artists alike, whereas Toronto was thought of as a puritanical provincial backwater – a boring, constipated place where you couldn't get wine with dinner. Post-colonial attitudes lingered on, and it was assumed that any first-rate cultural products were imported from abroad – from

Europe if you were old-fashioned, from New York if you thought of yourself as the cutting edge.

But for young writers, even young female writers, there were compensations to living in the sticks. Cultural trends are never as oppressively homogeneous in the outbacks as they are in the imperial centres, and in Canada there was a generation of women poets just before MacEwen's who hadn't yet heard that they were supposed to be non-creative by psychological fiat: Phyllis Webb, Anne Wilkinson, Jay Macpherson, P.K. Page and Margaret Avison. Also, the Canadian writing community then was so small, beleaguered and desirous of reinforcements that it was welcoming to any newcomer with talent, especially such an outstanding talent as MacEwen's.

It wasn't unusual for a young Canadian writer of that time to begin with poetry. Like many of her contemporaries, MacEwen eventually wrote novels and short stories, and during the course of her career she also produced radio plays, translations for the theatre and travel writing; but the poetry appeared first. For most of the 1960s, poetry was the predominant literary form in Canada: the few existing publishers were reluctant to take chances with new novelists, as novels were expensive to publish and were thought to have a limited audience inside Canada, and none at all outside it. But poems could be published as broadsheets, or in one of the five or six 'little' magazines then extant, or by one of the small presses; or they could be broadcast on the radio – notably on the CBC's pivotal programme, 'Anthology'. Or, since poetry readings had just recently become popular, they could be read aloud.

I first met Gwendolyn MacEwen in the autumn of 1960, at The Bohemian Embassy, a Toronto coffee house that featured jazz and folk singing and, once a week, poetry readings. The Embassy had the décor of its period – the checked tablecloths, the black walls, the candles in chianti bottles; it was also a smoke-filled firetrap. But it was a mecca to the poetry community, and MacEwen, who was nineteen by then, was already a regular reader there. She was a slight-figured, doe-eyed girl with long dark hair, who read in a surprisingly assured sultry and caressing voice. The combination of the child-like appearance, the rich voice and the poetic authority were compelling – many who remember these evenings testify that they went away from a MacEwen reading feeling they'd been let in on a unique and delicious secret.

MacEwen's primary interest as a poet was in language, and in its corollary, myth-making. In this she was not alone: the period comprised a sort of minor Age of Myth, though there were, of course, other influences at work. Northrop Frye's *Anatomy of Criticism* held critical centre-stage; Marshall McLuhan and his structural analysis of culture were beginning to make an impact. Leonard Cohen's first collection was called *Let Us Compare Mythologies*; James Reaney's magazine *Alphabet* – for which MacEwen wrote – was devoted to the correspon-dences between 'real life' and 'story'; and Canadian poets were endlessly telling one another that what they really needed to do was to create an 'indigenous mythology'. In this context, MacEwen's interest in the mythic structuring of reality – in opposition to the disappointing world of mundane experience she often refers to as 'Kanada' – seems less bizarre. She had an intense interest in Ancient Egypt and the Middle East, but her imaginative other-world is not limited to one time or place. In general – and especially in her earlier poetry – she opposes the works of children, magicians, adventurers, escape artists, the hierarchical and splendid past, the divinely mad, the 'barbaric', and poetry, to that of grown-ups, materialists, bureaucrats, the modern daily grind, stolid sanity, the 'tame', and newspaper prose. As she herself said, 'Poets are magicians without quick wrists.'

One of the paradoxes of MacEwen's work is that the protagonists or personae that she chooses are almost invariably male. She speaks in a female voice when addressing, as the lyric 'I', a male 'you', but when she uses a more dramatic form, or writes a poem about a heroic figure, the central character is usually a man, such as the escape artist Manzini, or Sir John Franklin, or – in a later, major work – Lawrence of Arabia. When female figures from history or story do appear as speakers, they are likely to be exceptions to their sex, such as an Egyptian princess, or Rider Haggard's She, with her supernatural powers.

This isn't really surprising. In view of her childhood experience with her mother – a mother whom she could neither forget nor renounce – MacEwen's relationship to women was problematic; but even aside from that, the roles available to women at the time lacked energy. What interested her were risk and exploration; thus the choice of a male voice was almost inevitable. She was entranced with cosmic predicaments, and the time for female astronauts had not yet come. Power – including the darker side of power – was much more interesting to her than powerlessness. She might have analysed the female condition and then tapped the resulting anger, like Anne Sexton; but then she would have been a very different kind of poet.

In the love poems she does assume a female voice, but she uses it to invoke and extol what appears to be a transcendent male figure, a kind of male Muse. However, it's evident who is doing the invoking, and in invocation, success is dependent on the verbal skill of the conjuror. In her poetry, MacEwen chooses to be female only when she can also choose the status of priestess. Her poems are – considering her life – surprisingly free from accusation, mourning and self-pity. Although in her later work she turns away from the mountain-climbing of her youth and descends further and further into the shadowy underworld, it is in search of confrontation: 'There is something down there and you want it told.' Still, what primarily engaged her was not complaint but exuberance, and a defiant celebration: praise in the face of darkness. Or, as she herself put it: 'Deal, infidel, the night is indeed difficult.'

I have divided this selection of her poems into five sections, which are arranged chronologically. Her first two booklets, *Selah* and *The Drunken Clock*, were self-published, which was usual for young poets at the time. Her first major collection, *The Rising Fire* (1963), was published by Contact Press, a well-known poet-run house, and contains some of the poems from the two earlier pamphlets. In the same year – when she was a mere twenty-two – she also published a novel, *Julian the Magician*. At the time she commented, 'I still feel extremely embryonic.'

A Breakfast for Barbarians appeared in 1966, from Ryerson Press. By this time she had married her first husband, poet Milton Acorn – a good many years her senior – but was already pursuing a divorce. Financially, her life was still precarious, as it would continue to be for most of her life; her dream of earning a living through historical fiction was never realised.

A Breakfast for Barbarians was greeted with much enthusiasm, and many regard it as her single most accomplished collection. Of it, she wrote:

These poems arise out of a wilful hunger, a deep involvement with self and world, a belief that to live consciously is holy, while merely to exist is sacrilege . . .

Here is a book of poems – or call it a menu. A breakfast menu, breakfast being a more profound and sacramental meal than supper, because after all it's the first meal; it's the pact you make with yourself to see the day through.

I should like to think these poems have a certain value for what I term their essential 'optimism' . . . I write basically to communicate joy, mystery, passion, not the joy that naively exists without knowledge of pain, but that joy which arises out of and conquers pain. I want to construct a myth.

Section II contains *Terror and Erebus*, one of the verse plays MacEwen wrote for radio in the early 1960s, and in my opinion the best. It's about the doomed Franklin expedition to the Arctic, and flows from another of her obsessions: men who venture into waste places. Deserts and emptiness always fascinated her.

Section III contains poems written between 1966 and 1972, and published in *The Shadow-Maker* (Macmillan, 1969), which won the Governor-General's Award, and *The Armies of the Moon* (Macmillan, 1972). During the same period she also published a volume of short stories, *Noman*, and a long novel based on the life of the Egyptian king Akhnaton. The sequence of poems, 'The Nine Arcana of the Kings', is connected with this second work.

The titles of the two books from which this section is drawn indicated the direction in which MacEwen's poetry was now taking: down rather than up, away from the exuberant fire and sparkle of her earlier work and towards a probing of the shadow side – the 'left hand' of nature and of the self – that had been present in her work from the beginning.

Another volume, *The Fire-Eaters*, appeared in 1976, but the work in it was not her best. Then there was a pause – her second and happier marriage, to a Greek singer with whom she ran a coffee house, was breaking up. Although earlier terrified by alcohol, which had killed her father, she had now begun to drink too much, although intermittently. However, in 1982 she published *The T.E. Lawrence Poems* (Mosaic Press), an astonishing sequence based on the ambiguous desert hero. Lawrence had been a lifelong obsession for MacEwen; she saw him as her twin, another male Muse, another uncertain mystic, and another lover of deserts and emptiness.

The poems in Section V are from *Afterworlds* (McClelland and Stewart, 1987), which appeared seven months before her death. Hindsight has perfect vision, but all the same the title is creepily prophetic; and MacEwen had been told by the doctors that if she continued to drink she was dicing with death. Many of these poems are either retrospective or elegiac; it was as if she was looking back over what she had done and what had happened to her, to decide whether or not she wanted it to go on. She was never suicidal in any conventional sense; but as a little girl she had wanted to be Mary Marvel, and had almost jumped off a cliff wearing a satin bed-jacket for a cloak, in the belief that she ought to be able to fly. There was a part of her that liked to challenge fate.

In the thirty years of her writing life, Gwendolyn MacEwen created a complete and diverse poetic universe and a powerful and unique voice, by turns playful, extravagant, melancholy, daring and profound. In the best of her poems, her range and craft, her poetic strength and intelligence, speak for themselves. To read her remains an exacting but delightful pleasure, though not one without its challenges and shadows. She remains unique.

Margaret Atwood, 1966

I.

From *The Drunken Clock, The Rising Fire*
and *A Breakfast for Barbarians*
1961–6

CERTAIN FLOWERS

some unthinking god
threw me cold violets last morning
when the rain was a prince in the garden.

said: here, define a certain fear in flowers,
chalk out quickly the peril of beauty,

said softly this, as I worried private light
among the blooms
and stretched a half-winged bird of verse
to band the prince, the bloodless blossoms.

some unthinking god
is made of towering flowers; his eye
in the tall blue tulip sky,
a profound petal there; I arrest its blooming.

!I want the flowers beheaded,
the garden sink,
the rain deny its claim to princedom there

and stand in a garden of void
applauding, tracing the biographies
of brief past flowers, capturing the moment of bloom
in a cage of my own sunlight

THE BREAKFAST

under the knuckles of the warlord sun how long do we have
how long do we have, you ask, in the vast magenta wastes
of the morning world when the bone buckles under for war
when the bone intersects as tangents in the district of the sun
centipedes and infidels; snakes and the absence of doves?

a breakfast hysteria; perhaps you have felt it,
the weight of the food you eat, the end of the meal coming
before you lift the spoon; or eat only apples
to improvise an eden. or forget the end takes place
in each step of your function.

look, the spoon is lifted halfway through invisible tables
of dangerous logarithms in the abstract morning spaces;
come, come – eat leviathans in the breakfast wastelands
eat bestiaries and marine zoos and apples and aviaries.
by eating the world you may enclose it.

seek simplicities; the fingerprints of the sun only
and the fingernail of the moon duplicating you in your body,
the cosmos fits your measures; has no ending;

place one hand before the sun and make it smaller,
hold the spoon in your hand up to the sky
and marvel at its relative size; comfort yourself
with the measures of a momentary breakfast table.

ah lord sun
ah terrible atomic breakfast
ah twilight of purple fallout
ah last deck of evening cards –
deal, infidel the night is indeed difficult

THE MOUNTAIN: A STUDY IN RELATIVE REALITIES

the staccato from the gut
like sunset guns, the way we stutter
cryptic causalities and command queer reasons
for mountains based on smashed senses – eyes
like screens, ears like blocked harbors, skulls
like tonal caves which echo altogether too much
and hearts like red whales behind the fishbone ribs
which are boorish and stupid and fly our brains
like kites

is too much. Ah
in our weird apocalyptic sceneries, whimsies
and filigreed senses define little after all;
a mountain is an inviolate triangle in an offhand
way, vaguely difficult to handle in a manual
sense, but our sunset faces are sweet landscapes
with rosy retinae and receptive nostrils and
it is too soon to think of halfway vision and
the questions of perception of an inverted people
etcetera.

The mountain . . . say
imagine we could double it or make an octave
of mountain or generally manipulate things concave
or convex or whatever, an amusing distraction
like war or dominoes, though somewhere the point
is lost. But now you watch me through your sunset
senses for you expected a poem and prose is suggested.
O men mouthing staccato causalities, O women with
queer cryptic reasons for all things – I grant
it is difficult in these equivocal Canadian sunsets

to imagine that through your senses you do indeed
       invent the mountain.
           Anyhow, absurd,
    but it does serve literature.
Anyone for tea before the night falls?

Universe And: The Electric Garden

the protons and the neutrons move, gardener,
sire their sons, spirals of sense,
and servant their planets,
their negative pebbles
in a pool of moons; electrons like
mad bees
        circle;
           · the nuclei reach out
to harness them;
           will of the sun reach out,
strap earth, strap moon, slowly excite
other stars, set, set the sweet fanatic pace
going;
      telescopes turn inward, bend down.

In our gardens are electric roses
which spark, push light, push fuchsia
in flailing grass

and spines of long magnetic seas cloy . . .
rake their depths for dust; all holds;
the spines hold the elemental jelly
of the sea's; flesh there . . .

I walk warily through
my electric garden

THE DIMENSIONS OF A TIGER

the cat in the grass lengthens –
and your tendons reach widely
into seasons of wind and deltas –
you are suddenly aware that
you have no boundaries, that
you are a field with no fences.

hollyhock and frolic, you
are the width of wind and voices
until something, a microscopic irony
as laughter breaking from windows
or a diminutive rain shrinks you
and the cat in the grass curls under

MORNING LAUGHTER

To my mother, Elsie MacEwen

umbilical I lumbered
trailing long seed, unwombed
to the giant vagina, unarmed,
no sprung Athene
– cry, cry in the sudden salt
of the big room, world
– I uncurled plastic limbs of senses,
freed the crashing course of menses,
                              – hurled

I hurled the young tongue's spit
for a common coming, a genesis
sans trumpets and myrrh, rejected
whatever seed in love's inside
fought and formed me from
an exodus of semen come
      for the dream of Gwen,
      the small one,
      whose first salt scream
heralded more and borrowed excellence.

years have tied the sweet cord;
morning laughter, ships of daughter
and of mother move together
in clumsy grace:
you look to a roof of brass clouds
crash loud as the known world knows us;
and each motion's intrinsic as I reach
beyond roofs for a clutch of that first seed.

wary we speak from a fringe of meanings,
circle and pat-a-cake in cat-paw diplomacy,
each hope hoisted to a veined rainbow,
our common denominator, whose colors
are all blood and bone,

wary we speak from a fringe of meanings,
each tongue censored with love and its
cat-paw circling
        ,now foetal in the world's wide womb
        ,now known in my own rebellious belly
        the stuff to people further days
        ,now forced by some grim reason
        to hark down the bonds of the blood
        ,can still remember from that womb walking,
        sideways out of that womb,
        glorious from that womb, bent and insolent.

– morning laughter with your young daughter –
smile at the pen she picks, armed to bring light
into terrible focus
and the paper builds worlds but makes
no prodigal . . .

who would erase the scribbled slate
of gone years, their jumbled algebra,
their rude designs
junked under a rainbow, all blood and bone
that links the mother and the morning daughter –
and acknowledge now, armed and still insolent

that what is housed in the fragile skull
– light or learning or verbal innocence –
grows from the woman somehow who housed the whole
body,
who first fed the vessels, the flesh and the sense.

For Alick MacEwen: d. 1960

what we have left behind us in the fathering clay
the finishing bed where the veins flow grey
in the grave unequivocal, is little, redundancy.

long long beneath the morning moon of our halfway
vision, our wrong repent repeats, stalls
the noon coming, is wrong recalling.

(stolen stolen by the thieves of gravity,
the inverse womb, the inward worm, etc.
O God forgive us these, etc.)

but say you chase life the way you chase
the sunset in grey jets on sunday still
though an organist's veins are opening

for the last warm music; you
were classic somewhere in Canada on sunday
touching trees where old apples fall and birds occur –

(give us that particular cruelty necessary
to take it, your life, a second time, it is
time to speak the truth, it is time to speak,
it is time)

THE CATALOGUES OF MEMORY

1.

now in our distorted distances
the ignorant ships
kiss
and pass

love we have learned nothing
we have learned
nothing
not in the slated nights
not in the chalkboard cities

Jesus, Nietsche, call them
and they will not come for you
though your hair is on fire
from the brain beneath it burning

love we have learned nothing
we have learned
nothing
not on the gold island
not on the washed beaches

we were two ships of burning glass
we were two ships of burning glass

now in our distorted distances
the ignorant ships
kiss
and pass

2.

endangered
you
the strokes of the sun were
lashes to your lips your
brow
beauty burning in
the fires of your room

ah what do I speak
I with pencils
what do I speak
who love you
under fire and churches
in snow
in rainlight
even behind the seasons

sunday somewhere you were
red and gold on beaches
disturbed with gulls
and steamers

monday somewhere you were
gay among ruins
old stone the fake
architecture of Kingsmere
dancing the colors were
Fall the colors fell
into your hair into

your brow etc.

ah who am I with pencils
who love you
behind reason
behind the poem
even behind the seasons
defining as the poem pillages
reason, you who defy the reasons
of poetry, you endangered
by your own images

3.

your hand on my left breast
perhaps, or the ankles
staying; the genitals like tears;
your eyes wide with fear.
the attack.
lions . . . the lean loins of them,
we were ships we were lions, we
were delicate with our images,
we were man in a blind man's vision
and our name was adam and we had no home.

always always was your face moving
before the ships before the buildings,
a crescent leaning, the conscience
of the flesh.

now it is winter; heed, heed
I say, heed
the speech of your hands.
feet, feet, I say,

move swiftly,
leave
no track

THE CHOICE

and so we have a choice of several deaths.

death one, the catapult farflung wish
        from the stomach or the skullcave
        shot like a bat out of belfries
        or various hells, like a horse
        through a landscape of cardboard
        calendars.

death two, it is lovely, it is lovely
        the second death, you
        do not even know it, you
        just fold up on a subway
        like yesterday's newspaper
        until someone picks you up
        not bothering to read you.

death three, it is dirty, it is dirty
        the third death because
        you plan it. it offends
        people, it is offensive, a car
        from a cliff, a hole behind
        the eyes, a drug dream.

and so we have a choice of several deaths
and that in itself is a consolation.
so go to it love, go to it:
the red of the flower your fingers are holding,
the green in the speech of your mouth;
drive it, drive the horse through landscapes

like calendars of cardboard, or nonsense mosaics
for we are great statements in our days

and on the basis of that we can expect small audiences.

A Breakfast for Barbarians

my friends, my sweet barbarians,
there is that hunger which is not for food –
but an eye at the navel turns the appetite
round
with visions of some fabulous sandwich,
the brain's golden breakfast

                      eaten with beasts
                      with books on plates

let us make an anthology of recipes,
let us edit for breakfast
our most unspeakable appetites –
let us pool spoons, knives
and all cutlery in a cosmic cuisine,
let us answer hunger
with boiled chimera
and apocalyptic tea,
an arcane salad of spiced bibles,
tossed dictionaries –

                      (O my barbarians
                      we will consume our mysteries)

and can we, can we slake the gaping eye of our desires?
we will sit around our hewn wood table
until our hair is long and our eyes are feeble,
eating, my people, O my insatiates,
eating until we are no more able
to jack up the jaws any longer –

to no more complain of the soul's vulgar cavities,
to gaze at each other over the rust-heap of cutlery,

drinking a coffee that takes an eternity –
till, bursting, bleary,
we laugh, barbarians, and rock the universe –
and exclaim to each other over the table
over the table of bones and scrap metal
over the gigantic junk-heaped table:

by God that was a meal

THE GARDEN OF SQUARE ROOTS:

An Autobiography

and then the rattlesnake spines of men distracted me
for even they, the people were
as Natajara was, who danced
while I was anchored like a passive verb
or Neptune on a subway –

and from the incredible animal i
grew queer claws inward to fierce cribs;
I searched gardens for square roots,
for i was the I interior
the thing with a gold belt and delicate ears
with no knees or elbows
was working from the inside out

this city I live in I built with bones
and mortared with marrow;
I planned it in my spare time
and its hydro is charged from a blood niagara
and I built this city backwards and
the people evolved out of the buildings
and the subway uterus ejected them –

for i was the I interior
the thing with a gold belt and delicate ears
with no knees or elbows
was working from the inside out.

and all my gardens grew backwards
and all the roots were finally square
and Ah! the flowers grew there like algebra

THE HOUSE

in this house poems are broken,
I would invent the end of poetry;
we are only complete when

> that image of me in you
> that image of you in me
> breaks, repairs itself.

you are the earth and the earth;
release those cosmic hands which held you
while I set out on my urgent journeys –

> in this house we repair
> torn walls together and do not
> ask how they were torn.

we work slowly, for
the house is the earth
and the earth –

> the delicate people in you
> move
> from room to room.

It Rains, You See

Reader, I do not want to complicate the world
but mathematics is tragic, there is pathos in numbers;
it's all over, boys – space is curved,
you are hungry and your hunger multiplies by hundreds.

in your first shuddering temple of chalk
in the slate days you taught numbers
to jive under the complex chewing pencils; you talked
darkly of the multiplying world, and your fingers

hunted for braille like urgent forms.
you go outside and now it rains,
and the rain is teaching itself its own name;
it rains, you see, but Hell it comes down cuneiform.

STRANGE BREAKFAST

I have eaten
strange breakfasts
with you.

Insatiate. These breakfasts
have broken the past
of smashed appetites;
that colossal intake
of morning images
has made me insatiate (ah you
and your colored hungers
who doth enclose my life and my death
in your coffee – friend,
we cannot live too long)

obviously we are preparing for some final feast,
obviously our bellies stretch
for a supreme reason, obviously
we can stomach anything now, anything.

that these breakfasts have broken the past
hungers, hungers that were controlled,
controlled hungers, that these breakfasts
have broken them, that everyone does not wish
executed fish and fried eggs,
that the full belly means only
a further hunger, that we cannot now return
to younger appetites, that we can no longer
eat the bright ancestral food,
that we alone must set all our tables single-handed,

that we alone must account for the grease of our spoons
that we alone must wash our mouths
that we alone must look back and decline
all dinner offers,
that we alone will walk into the city at 9 o'clock
knowing that the others have also eaten
knowing that there is no time to compare the contents
of our bodies in our cities
that we eat and we eat and we know and we know
that machines work faster than the machines of our mouths

is why our breakfasts
get stranger and stranger.

You Cannot Do This

you cannot do this to them, these are my people;
I am not speaking of poetry, I am not speaking of art.
you cannot do this to them, these are my people.
you cannot hack away the horizon in front of their eyes.

the tomb, articulate, will record your doing,
I will record it also, this is not art,
this is a kind of science, a kind of hobby,
a kind of personal vice like coin collecting.

it has something to do with horses
and signet rings and school trophies,
it has something to do with the pride of the loins,
it has something to do with good food and music,
and something to do with power, and dancing.
you cannot do this to them, these are my people.

THE CHILDREN ARE LAUGHING

It is monday and the children are laughing
The children are laughing; they believe they are princes
They wear no shoes; they believe they are princes
And their filthy kingdom heaves up behind them

The filthy city heaves up behind them
They are older than I am, their feet are shoeless
They have lived a thousand years; the children are laughing
The children are laughing and their death is upon them

I have cried in the city (the children are laughing)
I have worn many colors (the children are laughing)
They are older than I am, their death is upon them
I will wear no shoes when the princes are dying

POEM IMPROVISED AROUND A FIRST LINE*

the smoke in my bedroom which is always burning
worsens you, motorcycle Icarus;
you are black and leathery and lean and
you cannot distinguish between sex and nicotine

anytime, it's all one thing for you –
cigarette, phallus, sacrificial fire –
all part of that grimy flight
on wings axlegreased from Toronto to Buffalo
for the secret beer over the border –

now I long to see you fullblown and black
over Niagara, your bike burning and in full flame
and twisting and pivoting over Niagara
and falling finally into Niagara,
and tourists coming to see your black leather wings
hiss and swirl in the steaming current –

now I long to give up cigarettes
and change the sheets on my carboniferous bed;
O baby, what Hell to be Greek in this country
without wings, but burning anyway

*The first line around which it was improvised has disappeared.

THE LEFT HAND AND HIROSHIMA

asked once why I fanned my fingers before my eyes
to screen the strange scream of them, I, sinister, replied:
Recently I dropped a bomb upon Hiroshima.

as for the mad dialectics of my tooth-chewed hands
I knew nothing; the left one was responsible and
abominably strong, bombed the flower of Hiroshima.

only because my poems are lies do they earn the right
to be true, like the lie of that left hand at night
in the cockpit of a sad plane trailing God in its wake.

all the left hands of your bodies, your loud thumbs
did accomplice me! men women children at the proud womb,
we have accomplished Hell. Woe Hiroshima . . .

you have the jekyll hand you have the hyde hand
my people, and you are abominable; but now I am in proud and
in uttering love I occur four-fingered and garbed
in a broken gardener's glove over the barbed
                garden
                of Hiroshima . . .

POEM

the slow striptease of our concepts
        – it is even this which builds us,
for you I would subtract my images
        for the nude truth beneath them

as you, voluptuous, as with mirrors at the loins
        are unclothed piece by piece until
each cloth is slander to your skin and
        nakedness itself is silk across your rising sex

SUBLIMINAL

in that sublayer of sense
where there is no time
no differentiation of identities
but co-presents, a static recurrence
(that wolf is stone,
this stone is wolf)

your bones have interlocked
behind my brow
your meanings are absolute
you do not move
but are always moving

in that substratum I hold,
unfold you at random;
your eye is a giant
overflowing me;
your foot is planted
in the marrow of my bone,
today is tomorrow.

vision does not flinch
perspective is not jarred
you do not move
but are always moving

you do not move but are always moving
Christ O Christ no one lives long
along that layer;
I rise to see you planted

in an earth outside me,
moving through time
through the terms of it,
moving through time again
along its shattered latitudes

THE BEAD SPECTRUM

you laugh you cry you wear bright beads
and the colors love you, dozens
huddle upon you.

O lady, the world will not confess your colors
and nowhere are your beads acknowledged
against the spectrum of your city.

but your beads love you
and form their own spectrum
and your fingers fumble them
(infra-red to your throat's final violet)
as colors clash
and all the world's unspeakable accessories
shake like a stripper's machines
and its large horny music
exits you to nakedness.

now in your plural world
your colors huddle, confess themselves
upon your flesh (a pallid apocalypse) –
dynamos crash, and in your room sewing,
you laugh you cry you wear bright beads.

THE PEANUT BUTTER SANDWICH

we are dangerous at breakfast, at breakfast we
        investigate the reasons for our myths
viciously, and at breakfast we need no reasons
        for being; we are

solemnly eating our thick sandwiches
        and knowing the highest mysticism
is this courageous breakfast and us at it
        concentrating
        conscious

of our outrageous reality. The sandwich!
        The peanut butter sandwich!
a symbol of itself only, and you beautiful
        across the table, eating.

but caught in this cliché of a breakfast
        and knowing it too, we speak
loudly: 'Feed me some symbolisms!
        I want a dragon sandwich!'

'I am freight train, sea-wind and raspberry jam!'
'I am snow, tiger and peanut butter!'

alas, we have too many myths
        and we know that too. but it is breakfast.
I am with you. care for another?

THE MAGICIAN

for Raymond Lowe

finally then the hands must play mad parables
finally then, the fingers' genius
wave out what my poems have said;
finally then must the silks occur

                              plus rabbits

and the big umbrellas be
spun on stage continually.

as you Lowe, in quiet irony
inspire terrible skills of silks

                    or crash scarves vertically

as though miniature brains were held in fingertips
fantastic as of secrecy –

or my art being more a lie anyway
than the lie of these illusions
secreting realities in the twitching silks
or sacred sleeves

                    to twist or tamper them

to come out solid, in cubes or cups –
pull down then

                    silk avalanche of scarves

or play the cosmos on strings of human hair

                    as a wand cracks

and blinds belief and holds it knotted
        like an ugly necklace
        or a hopeless rope –

or you, Lowe, driving a spike through the head of a boy
as though magic were (and is)
a nail of steel to split the skull

                                    in either direction
to believe or not believe
is not the question.

finally then do all my poems become as crazy scarves
issuing from the fingers in a colored mesh
and you, magician, stand as they fly around you
silent as Houdini who could escape from anything
except the prison of his own flesh.

Manzini: Escape Artist

now there are no bonds except the flesh; listen –
there was this boy, Manzini, stubborn with
gut stood with black tights and a turquoise
leaf across his sex

and smirking while the big
brute tied his neck arms legs, Manzini
naked waist up and white with sweat

struggled. Silent, delinquent, he
was suddenly all teeth and knee, straining slack
and excellent with sweat, inwardly

wondering if Houdini would take as long
as he; fighting time and the drenched
muscular ropes, as though his tendons were worn
on the outside –

as though his own guts were the ropes
encircling him; it was beautiful. it was thursday; listen –
there was this boy, Manzini

finally free, slid as snake from
his own sweet agonized skin, to throw his entrails
white upon the floor
with a cry of victory –

now there are no bonds except the flesh,
but listen, it was thursday, there was this boy,
Manzini –

THE THING IS VIOLENT

Self, I want you now to be
violent and without history,
for we've rehearsed too long our ceremonial ballet
and I fear my calm against your exquisite rage.

I do not fear that I will go mad
but that I may not, and the shadows of my sanity
blacken out your burning; act once
and you need not act again –
give me no ceremony, scars are not pain.

The thing is violent, nothing precedes it,
it has no meaning before or after –
sweet wounds which burn like stars,
stigmata of the self's own holiness,
appear and plot new zodiacs upon the flesh.

APPENDECTOMY

it's interesting how you can brag about a scar;
I'm fascinated with mine; it's diagonal and straight,
it suggests great skill, great speed,
it is no longer or shorter than it needs to be.

it is good how it follows my natural symmetry
parallel to the hip, a perfect geometry;
it is not a wound; it is a diagram
drawn correctly, it has no connection with pain.

it's interesting how you can brag about a scar;
nothing in nature is a straight line
except this delightful blasphemy on my belly;
the surgeon was an Indian, and beautiful, and holy.

FINALLY LEFT IN THE LANDSCAPE

Finally left in the landscape is the dancer;
    all maps have resigned, the landscape has
designed him. My lines can only
    plagiarize his dance.

    Moving, he is the cipher of movement,
    a terrific code,
    witness him.

Now I seek him, nor rely on chance,
I turn stones and find broken glass
like pseudo-suns in the broken sand
intense for their size
(are they from his fallen eyes?)

Life, your trillions people me,
I am a continent, a violated geography,
Yet still I journey to this naked country
to seek a form which dances in the sand.
This is my chosen landscape.
Hear my dark speech, deity.

THE ARISTOCRACIES

You are born with these in your blood –
natural aristocracies, not power aristocracies
as the world sees them, but natural aristocracies
evident from the curve of the mouth, from the stance.

The title you confer upon yourself, a pre-occupation
with eagles, a passion for gold, for mountains
for that which is super-natural, superlative,
grants you your maps and your kingdoms.

Let it be understood, this is not art,
this is not poetry; the poetry is
the breathing air embracing you,
the poetry is not here, it is elsewhere
in temples, in territories of pure blue.

Behind my eye a diagonal arabic music
insists I censure dimensions; I think
in cross-sections of sound, flat arabesques;
love, I think you have become a bas-relief.

Can you not break from this censured landscape?
I waste each blue breath from my mouth
and I cannot recover the exiled minutes of my life –
(ruthless, and royal blue the profiles of kings
confound me)

The body of God and the body of you
dance through the same diagonal instant
of my vision. Let this be the end of argument,

O crowned and captive dancer, let me not argue
your flesh to death.

You must dance forever beneath this heavy crown
in an aristocratic landscape, a bas-relief of living bone.
And I will altogether cease to speak
as you do a brilliant arabesque within the bas-relief,
your body bent like the first letter
of an unknown, flawless alphabet.

II.

Terror and Erebus:
A Verse Play for Radio

TERROR AND EREBUS

The Speakers –
> RASMUSSEN
> FRANKLIN
> CROZIER
> QAQORTINGNEQ

(*Roaring wind which fades out to Rasmussen*)

RASMUSSEN:

King William Island . . . latitude unmentionable.
But I'm not the first here.
They preceded me, they marked the way
         with bones
White as the ice is, whiter maybe,
The white of death,
         of purity . . .

But it was almost a century ago
And sometimes I find their bodies
Like shattered compasses, like sciences
Gone mad, pointing in a hundred directions
         at once –
The last whirling graph of their agony.
How could they know what I now know,
A century later, my pockets stuffed with
         comfortable maps –
That this was, after all, an island,
That the ice can camouflage the straits
And drive men into false channels,

Drive men

into white, sliding traps . . .?

How could they know, even stand back and see
The nature of the place they stood on,
When no man can, no man knows where he stands
Until he leaves his place, looks back
        and knows.

Ah, Franklin! I would like to find you
Now, your body spreadeagled like a star,
A human constellation in the snow.
                The earth insists
There is but one geography, but then
There is another still –
The complex, crushed geography of men.
You carried all maps within you;
Land masses moved in relation to
                you –
As though you created the Passage
By willing it to be.
                Ah, Franklin!
To follow you one does not need geography.
At least not totally, but more of that
Instrumental knowledge the bones have,
Their limits, their measurings.
The eye creates the horizon,
The ear invents the wind,
The hand reaching out from a parka sleeve
By touch demands that the touched thing
                be.

(*Music and more wind sound effects, fade out*)

RASMUSSEN:

So I've followed you here
Like a dozen others, looking for relics
                of your ships, your men.
Here to this awful monastery
                where you, where Crozier died,
                and all the men with you died,
Seeking a passage from imagination to
                reality,
Seeking a passage from land to land
                by sea.

Now in the arctic night
I can almost suppose you did not die,
But are somewhere walking between
The icons of ice, pensively
                like a priest,
Wrapped in the cold holiness of snow,
                of your own memory . . .

(*Music bridge to Franklin, wind sound effects*)

FRANKLIN:

I brought them here, a hundred and twenty-nine men,
Led them into this bottleneck,
This white asylum.
I chose the wrong channel and
The ice folded in around us,
Gnashing its jaws, folded in
                around us . . .

The ice clamps and will not open.
For a year it has not opened
Though we bash against it
Like lunatics at padded walls.

My ships, The Terror, The Erebus
Are learning the meanings of their
                                names.
What madman christened them
The ships of Terror and of Hell?
In open sea they did four knots;
Here, they rot and cannot move at all.

Another winter in the ice,
The second one for us, folds in.
Latitude 70 N. November 25,1846.
The sun has vanished.

(*Music, etc.*)

RASMUSSEN:

Nothing then but to sit out the darkness,
The second sterile year,
                and wait for spring
And pray the straits would crack
Open, and the dash begin again;
Pray you could drive the ships
Through the yielding, melting floes,
                drive and press on down
Into the giant virginal strait of
                Victoria.
But perhaps she might not yield,
She might not let you enter,
                but might grip

And hold you crushed forever in her stubborn
                    loins,
                    her horrible house,
Her white asylum in an ugly marriage.

(*Music, etc.*)

FRANKLIN:

I told him, I told Crozier
The spring is coming, but it's wrong
                    somehow.
Even in summer the ice may not open,
It may not open.
Some of the men have scurvy, Crozier . . .
                    Their faces, the sick ones,
                    their faces reflect their minds.
I can read the disease in their souls.
It's a mildewed chart
On their flesh.
                    But this is no place
To talk of souls; here
The soul becomes the flesh.

(*Sighs*)

I may have to send men on foot
To where the passage is,
To prove it, to prove it is there,
That Simpson joins Victoria,
That there is a meaning, a pattern
                    imposed on this chaos,
A conjunction of waters,
                    a kind of meaning
Even here, even in this place . . .

RASMUSSEN:

A kind of meaning, even here,
Even in this place.
                    Yes, yes,
We are men, we demand
That the world be logical, don't we?

But eight of your men went overland
                    and saw it, proved it,
Proved the waters found each other
Laughs briefly, bitterly
                    as you said,
Saw the one – owing into the other,
Saw the conjunction, the synthesis
                    of faith, there
In the white metallic cold.

And returned to tell you, Franklin,
And found you dying in Erebus,
In the hell
                    of your body,
The last ship of your senses.

        June 11,1847 . . .

(*Music and sound effect bridge*)

RASMUSSEN:

Crozier took command,
A scientist, understanding magnetism,
                    the pull of elements, but
The laws which attract and as easily repel
Could not pull him from the hell

of his science.

Crozier, what laws govern
This final tug of war
                    between life and death,
The human polarities . . .?
What laws govern these?
                    The ice
Is its own argument.

(*Music bridge*)

CROZIER:

It is September, the end of summer . . .

(*Laughs briefly, bitterly*)

Summer, there was no summer . . .
Funny how you go on using
                    the same old terms
Even when they've lost all meaning.

Two summers, and the ice has not melted.
Has the globe tipped? The axis slipped?
                    Is there no sense of season
Anywhere?

September 1847.
We await our *third* winter in the ice.

> On the word third *a chilling sound effect*

RASMUSSEN:

But the ice, wasn't it drifting south
Itself, like a ship, a ship within a
Ship?

CROZIER:

The ice is drifting south, but
            not fast enough.
It has time, it has more time than we
            have time;
It has eternity to drift south.
Ice doesn't eat, doesn't get scurvy,
Doesn't die, like my men are dying.

(*Music to suggest a time lapse*)

CROZIER:

April 1848. The winter is over.
Supplies to last three months only.
We are leaving the ships for good.

RASMUSSEN:

You went overland, then.
Overland, an ironic word . . .
How can you call this land?
                  It's the white teeth
Of a giant saw,
                  and men crawl through it
Like ants through an upright comb.
Overland. You set out from the ships
In a kind of horrible birth,
                  a forced expulsion

From those two wombs, solid at least,
Three-dimensional, smelling of wood
And metal and familiar things.

Overland . . .

(*Music bridge*)

CROZIER:

April 21,1848. Good Friday.
Our last day in the ships.
We pray, we sing hymns, there
                is nothing else to do.
We are all of us crucified
                before an ugly Easter.
Civilization . . . six hundred and seventy miles away.

On the words six hundred and seventy miles away *more chilling
sound effects*

CROZIER:

A hundred and five men left. Three months' supplies.
Our Father who art in heaven,
Hallowed be thy name . . .
                Six hundred and seventy miles to civilization,
Three months' supplies, a hundred and five men . . .
Give us this day our daily bread
and forgive us . . .
                scurvy among the men.
                We leave ship tomorrow.
Thy kingdom come, thy will be done . . .
                Six hundred and seventy miles to
                civilization . . .
For Thine is the kingdom, and the Power,

And the Glory . . .
Our Father
Our Father
Our Father

RASMUSSEN:

April 25, 1848. HMS Terror and
Erebus were deserted, having been beset
since the 12th of September 1846.
The officers and crew consisting of a hundred and five
souls under the command of Captain F. R.
Crozier landed here.
The total loss by deaths in the Expedition
has been to this date nine officers and
fifteen men.
So you pushed on, and sun and snow,
            that marriage of agonizing light
Assailed you.

(*Music bridge*)

CROZIER:

In the beginning God made the light
And saw that it was good . . .
            the light . . .
            and saw that it was good . . .

(*Eerie music*)

My men fall back, blinded,
                    clutching their scorched eyes!
Who ever said that Hell was darkness?
What fool said that light was good
                    and darkness evil?
In extremes, all things reverse themselves;
In extremes there are no opposites.

RASMUSSEN:

The naked eye dilates, shrinks,
Goes mad, cannot save itself.
You didn't even have those wooden slits
The eskimos wore
                    to censor the sun,
                    to select as much light
As the eye can bear.
Some science could have tamed the light
For you,
                    not hope, not prayer –
But pairs of simple wooden slits,
Only those, only those ridiculous
                    instruments
You need to keep the cosmos out.
I share your irony, Crozier,
That, and your despair . . .

CROZIER:

(*Breathing heavily while speaking*)

To select what we will and will not see,
To keep the cosmos out with layers of cloth
                    and strips of leather –
                    That's man, I suppose,

an arrogant beast. Whether
He is right or wrong is –

O Hell ! Look, Lord, look how
They fall back behind me!

(*Music bridge*)

CROZIER:

I sent thirty men back to the ships,
Thirty good men back to the Terror, the Erebus
         for food, somehow.
We can go blind but we must eat
         in the white waste.
Though all our senses fall apart
         we must eat
         we must still eat . . .

RASMUSSEN:

Thirty good men.
On the way back all of them but five
         died,
Knelt before the sun for the last time
         and died,
Knelt like priests in the whiteness
         and died,
         on their knees, died,
Or stretched straight out,
Or sitting in a brief stop
         which never ended,
         died.

It does not matter how.

Five made it back to the ships
And there, in the womb, in the
                    wooden hulls,
                    died.
Five who could not go back,
Who could not a second time
Bear the birth, the going out,
                    the expulsion
                        into pure worlds of ice.

(*Music bridge*)

The men do not return with food.
We push on, we cannot wait here.
The winds wait, the sun waits,
                    the ice waits, but
We cannot wait here;
                    to stop is to die
In our tracks,
                    to freeze like catatonics
In our static houses of bone.

Already we look like statues,
                    marbled, white.
The flesh and hair bleaches out;
                    we are cast in plaster.
The ice cannot bear the flesh of men,
The sun will not tolerate coloring;
                    we begin already
To move into the ice, to mimic it.
Our Father who art in heaven,
Our Father
Our Father

(Music, wind)

One night we saw Eskimos
And they were afraid;
They gave us a seal,
They ran away at night . . .

(More music, wind)

CROZIER:

(Slowly)

We have come two hundred miles from the ships,
We have come two hundred miles.
There are thirty men left.
It is the end, it is
The end . . .

(Wind, bridge to)

RASMUSSEN:

Now there was nothing more to do,
        no notes to write and leave in cairns,
        no measurements to take, no
Readings of any temperatures
        save the inner
Agony of the blood.
Now, Crozier, now you come
To the end of science.

CROZIER:

(*Speaking slowly, painfully*)

We scattered our instruments behind us,
                    and left them where they fell
Like pieces of our bodies, like limbs
We no longer had need for;
                    we walked on and dropped them,
                    compasses, tins, tools, all of them.
Now we come to the end of science . . .

Now we leave ciphers in the snow,
We leave our instruments in the snow.
It is the end of science.
What magnet do I know of
Which will pull us south . . .?
                    none,
                    none but the last inevitable
                    one.
Death who draws
Death who reaches out his pulling arms
And draws men in like filings
                    on paper.

This is the end of science.
We left it behind us,
A graph in the snow, a horrible cipher,
                    a desperate code.
And the sun cannot read, and the snow
                    cannot either.

(*Music, etc. suggesting death*)

61

No, Crozier, the sun cannot read
And the snow cannot either.
But men can, men like me who come
To find your traces, the pieces
Of your pain scattered in the white
               vaults of the snow.
Men like me who come and stand
               and learn
The agony your blood learned –
               how the body is bleached
And the brain itself turns
               a kind of pure, purged
               white.

And what happened to the ships –
It hurts to talk of it.
               The Eskimo, Qaqortingneq
Knows –
               let him tell of it . . .

(*Wind etc. bridge to Qaqortingneq, who speaks slowly, falteringly, with language difficulties*)

QAQORTINGNEQ:

I remember the day
When our fathers found a ship.
They were hunting seals,
And it was spring
And the snow melted around
The holes where the seals breathed . . .

(*Music*)

Far away on the ice
My fathers saw a strange shape,
A black shape, too great to be seals.
They ran home and told all the men
In the village,
And the next day all came to see
This strange thing . . .

It was a ship, and they moved closer,
And saw that it was empty,
That it had slept there for a long time.
My fathers had never seen white men,
And my fathers did not know about ships.
They went aboard the great ship

As though into another world,
Understanding nothing;
They cut the lines of the little boat
Which hung from the ship
And it fell broken to the ice;
They found guns in the ship
And did not understand
And they broke the guns
And used them for harpoons . . .

And they did not understand . . .

They went into the little houses
On the deck of the ship,
And found dead people in beds
Who had lain there a long time.
Then they went down, down
Into the hull of the great ship

And it was dark
And they did not understand the dark . . .

And to make it light they bored a hole
In the side of the ship,
But instead of the light,
The water came in the hole,
And flooded, and sank the ship,
And my fathers ran away,
And they did not understand . . .

(*Music*)

RASMUSSEN:

And the papers? Franklin's papers?
The ship's logs, the reports?

QAQORTINGNEQ:

Papers, O yes!

The little children found papers
In the great ship,
But they did not understand papers.
They played with them,
They ripped them up,
They threw them into the wind
Like birds . . .

(*Music*)

RASMUSSEN:

(*Laughing bitterly*)

Maybe they were right, –
What would papers mean to them?
                    cryptic marks, latitudes,
                    signatures, journals,
                    diaries of despair,
                    official reports
Nobody needs to read.
I've seen the real journals
You left us, you Franklin, you Crozier.
I've seen the skulls of your men
                    in the snow, their sterile bones
Arranged around cairns like
                    compasses,
Marking out all the latitudes
                    and longitudes
Of men.

(*Music*)

Now the great passage is open,
The one you dreamed of, Franklin,
And great white ships plough through it
Over and over again,
Packed with cargo and carefree men.
It is as though no one had to prove it
Because the passage was always there.
Or . . . is it that the way was invented,
Franklin?
                    that you cracked the passage open
With the forces of sheer certainty?
                    – or is it that you cannot know,

Can never know,
Where the passage lies
Between conjecture and reality . . .?

(*Music, fade out*)

III.

From *The Shadow-Maker* and
The Armies of the Moon
1966–72

POEM

It is not lost, it is moving forward always,
Shrewd, and huge as thunder, equally dark.
Soft paws kiss its continents, it walks
Between lava avenues, it does not tire.

It is not lost, tell me how can you lose it?
Can you lose the shadow which stalks the sun?
It feeds on mountains, it feeds on seas,
It loves you most when you are most alone.

Do not deny it, do not blaspheme it,
Do not light matches on the dark of its shores.
It will breathe you out, it will recede from you.
What is here, what is with you now, is yours.

THE DISCOVERY

do not imagine that the exploration
ends, that she has yielded all her mystery
or that the map you hold
cancels further discovery

I tell you her uncovering takes years,
takes centuries, and when you find her naked
look again,
admit there is something else you cannot name,
a veil, a coating just above the flesh
which you cannot remove by your mere wish

when you see the land naked, look again
(burn your maps, that is not what I mean),
I mean the moment when it seems most plain
is the moment when you must begin again

THE PORTAGE

We have travelled far with ourselves
and our names have lengthened;
         we have carried ourselves
on our backs, like canoes
in a strange portage, over trails,
insinuating leaves
and trees dethroned like kings,
         from water-route to
         water-route
seeking the edge, the end,
the coastlines of this land.

On earlier journeys we
were master ocean-goers
going out, and evening always found us
spooning the ocean from our boat,
         and gulls, undiplomatic
         couriers brought us
cryptic messages from shore
till finally we sealords vowed
we'd sail no more.

Now under a numb sky, somber
cumuli weigh us down;
the trees are combed for winter
and bears' tongues have melted
all the honey;
         there is a loud
suggestion of thunder;
subtle drums under
the candid hands of Indians

are trying to tell us
why we have come.

But now we fear movement
and now we dread stillness;
we suspect it was the land
that always moved, not our ships;
we are in sympathy with the fallen
trees; we cannot relate
        the causes of our grief.
We can no more carry
our boats our selves
over these insinuating trails.

Dark Pines Under Water

This land like a mirror turns you inward
And you become a forest in a furtive lake;
The dark pines of your mind reach downward,
You dream in the green of your time,
Your memory is a row of sinking pines.

Explorer, you tell yourself this is not what you came for
Although it is good here, and green.
You had meant to move with a kind of largeness,
You had planned a heavy grace, an anguished dream.

But the dark pines of your mind dip deeper
And you are sinking, sinking, sleeper
In an elementary world;
There is something down there and you want it told.

ARCANUM ONE: THE PRINCE

and in the morning the king loved you most
and wrote your name with a sun and a beetle
and a crooked ankh, and in the morning
you wore gold mainly, and the king adorned you
with many more names.

beside fountains, both of you slender
as women, circled and walked together
like sunrays circling water, both of you
slender as women wrote your names with
beetles and with suns, and spoke together
in the golden mornings.

and the king entered your body
into the bracelet of his name
and you became a living syllable
in his golden script, and your body
escaped from me like founting water
all the daylong.

but in the evenings you wrote my name
with a beetle and a moon, and lay upon me
like a long broken necklace which had fallen
from my throat, and the king loved you
most in the morning, and his glamorous love
lay lengthwise along us all the evening.

Arcanum Two: The Conspirator

my brother, you board the narrow boat and the river owns
    you
over and over; why do you sail like this between your sister
and the distant king? my chamber is full of politics
and hunger. why do you go to him? his chin is thin
and his thighs bulge. why do you go to the king your father?

your boat, your narrow boat goes forth each morning
and snouts of crocodiles worry the water.
why do you go each morning after
our bodies make narrow rivers together?

I know how you plot against the king your father
whose thighs flung you forth as from a salty river;
you will steal the crown which bulges from his head
and mount the thin throne which no one holds forever.

O do not go to the king our father
but stay in this house beside the worried river;
there are a thousand kingdoms yet to conquer
in the narrow nights when we lie together,
and the distant king on his thin and hungry throne
can neither live nor lie nor sing forever.

ARCANUM THREE: THE DEATH OF THE PRINCE

He was employed upon the marble floor
Between the fountain and the pillars.
  They looked for him, the silvery guards
  Sought him all daylong, and my brother
Did not hear them calling through the halls.

And finding him employed upon the marble floor
They fell before him crying: Majesty!
  (Lord, his mouth was terrible
  And his cheek a granite cliff)
And he lifted up his head and smiled.

He was destroyed upon the marble floor
Between the fountain and the pillars
  And I bent over him to call his name,
  His secret name whose syllables were thunder –
Then I took the heavy crown and threw it in the river.

Arcanum Four: The Embalming

along your body strips of gold unroll
your name which caused a kingdom's fall
and your wrapped ribs, my silent one,
refuse the sun, and down your legs run
legends of the night. in white cloth I wound you
in your final house beside the water
and I know the gates are locked forever,
the gates of light are locked forever
as my loins lock, as the river.

in white cloth bound, and blind
you breathe in death the winds of night
as the sweet stiff corpse of your petrified
sex points upward into heaven
in your tomb beside the river,
though the gates of light are locked forever,
the legs and lips of light are locked forever.

my fingers twice have traced
your name all down your flesh, and they
have dipped its signs in water.
now sleep my blind, my silent brother
as my womb locks, as the river,
your tomb a virgin by jackals sealed
and the gates of light are locked forever.

Arcanum Five: The Prayer

death is a snake on your smashed brow
but still I beg you to get up and go
beyond the drowning river where your crown lies
towards the sighing house of reeds where I
stand waiting in the hollow doorway of eternity.

O brother, from your tomb arise! your bones
are targets in a hunter's eyes, your soul
the naked arrow which he fires.

in the name of our father, by the ring he wore,
come touch this floor with feet that burned
a thousand times the grass between the river
and this fervent house.
as bird arise, as arrow! and tomorrow
let the strips of linen fall.
all your limbs are tombs of sorrow.
I beg you now, my silent brother
to crash those gates which are not locked forever.
O bless and break them ten times over!

ARCANUM SIX: THE CENTURIES

I waited two millennia in the house beside the river
calling to the north wind many times over,
and feeding doves, and laying fruit beside your tomb
which thieves and beggars stole by night in summer,
and burning prayers and perfume on the hungry altar.
elsewhere slept our mad forgotten father
and the land fell into wretchedness, and later
watersnakes and foreign boats profaned the river.

and sometimes you visited as bird the thirsty bed
where we had lain, and hovered above and said,
'I will come back in better forms than this,
my sister, but the gates are hard to break,
so hard to break you cannot know
and death is like the long sleep after love
when nothing can persuade the limbs to move.'

your tired wings were songs among the leaves
and on my thighs you left your shining, unreal seed.

and other centuries I do not try to count
with doves and thieves and moons appeared and went,
with stars that wrote strange warnings in the skies.
the eyes of many kingdoms closed, the palace was defiled
by princes with strange-colored eyes.

brother, I awaited the end of all the world.

ARCANUM SEVEN: THE RETURN

now as I wear around my neck a necklace
of a million suns, you come
undead, unborn, thou Ghost of the morning!

I notice that you wear our father's ring
but I must say no more
for the bed of ebony and straw
lies like a fallen song upon the floor
where last we left it, broken with love and bare.
the world will loathe our love of salt and fire
and none will let you call me sister here.

see how my body bears the mouthmarks made
in times long past, star-wounds in night unhealed;
since then it was a cave by jackals sealed.
but now my legs are once more cages
for a great far-flying bird, my breasts
small pyramids of love, my mouth
is empty of the dark wine of my waiting.

O tell me all the things you saw,
and call me sister,
and bless this bed of ebony and straw.

ARCANUM EIGHT: THE STORY

'sister, from the gates and fields of night I came
lured by your voice as it spoke my name
over water and fire, and the voice of him
who told me that his sun would burn forever.

'I'll tell you why I went each morning to the river
and sailed towards that old man on the throne.
his seed struggled in my reluctant thighs
and the ring on his hand was stone
and his eyes were the mirrors of the world
and he was the very lord of gold.

'so I went each morning to the king my father.
but all is told, I cannot tell another thing
about how his blood was the birth of my soul
and how with my own hands I killed the king, the king.

'now when the sun is born each day at dawn
I will lie along your body as a boat along a river
and place my soul a blazing ornament upon your breasts
and burn with my bones my name all down your flesh.
sister, by a dark love bound and blind
I touch you now, in this forbidden time
and my white robes of death unwind.'

Arcanum Nine: The Ring

I do not adorn you with any more names
for the living ghost of the king our father
hovers forever above our secret bed
like the royal hawk with wings outspread
on whose head the awful sun burns out
the many generations of our dreams.

and we are the end of his ancient line,
your seed a river of arrested time
whose currents bring the cursed crown
forever back to the foot of this bed –
the double crown of those who wear
the kingdoms of heaven and hell on their head.

the royal bird is blind in morning
and its glamorous wings will shade us
till the end of time. but O my brother
will you wear forever that stolen ring
which wounds your hand by night, and why
in your dreams do you go to the king, the king?

IV.

From *The T.E. Lawrence Poems*
1982

MY MOTHER

In Dublin they called her The Holy Viper; she helped God
        to erase all sins except her own.
Knowing her means I'll never make any woman a mother;
Let them find something else to devour besides
        their own children.
She didn't care for girls in the house, they weren't her.

I never let her see exactly who I was and what I loved,
        for she would understand, and then I
        would have to also. She was illegitimate
        like me; it ran in our blood.

I was a standing civil war for as long as I remember,
Trying to contain both her and my father, and now
        I am a castle that she lays siege to;
        she aspires to its tower.

The Arabs say that Mother Eve is a giant who stands
        three hundred feet tall;
        if I raise myself to my full height
Then I can see her, green and powerful, gazing at me still.

Our Child Which Art In Heaven

The child leads the parents on to bear him; he demands
        to be born. And I sense somehow that God
Is not yet born; I want to create Him.

If everything were finished, and we could say
        we'd given birth to stars, if we could say
Give over, it's done – all would be wild, and fair

But it is not yet over; it has not yet begun.

God is not yet born, and we await the long scream
        of His coming. We want the water to break
So we can say: *In the Beginning was the Word.*

Meanwhile, if one must die for something,
        there's nothing like a cross
        from which to contemplate the world.

THE LEGITIMATE PRINCE

I was a flea in the legitimate prince's bed, the bed
Of he-who-was-not-me, he who had the real birthright.
He wore noble clothes,

                    and saved every damsel in distress
Within a hundred miles. His eyes and his scabbard shone.

He-who-was-not-me showed no mercy and no fear for
        anything.
Lies glanced off his sword – shot light.

                        Terror swooned;
He answered to no one, and claimed the world as his own.

He never looks anyone in the eye for fear they would fall
Into the well of his gaze and drown there, thrashing around
        like the fools, the pipsqueaks they were,
And he wanted to spare them.

                  All colors admired him, God
admired him, God how I longed to become him.

But I was born on the wrong side of the bed, which made me
Prince of Nothing, and I fell off the edge of it into Hell.

My Half-Sisters

Like the legitimate prince, they were legitimate princesses,
        (my father was actually married to their mother) –
And I, their bastard half-brother, used to imagine them
Crocheting doilies and toiling over impossible needlepoint
        in shadowy alcoves where their purple dresses
        fluttered, and their powerful and secret minds
        made mock of me and my bastard brothers.

One half of them was one half of me; I never could fathom
        what that meant. They were forbidden to me
        by blood, yet I felt them lurking, waiting
        to devour me just beyond my door.
My ghostly half-sisters, beautiful and cruel, were fond
Of tea and blueberry scones at ten past five, talked
        incessantly of me, and slowly got older.

Now I think they might drop a stitch when someone comes –
        a visitor or a casual friend – and asks them
        if their half-brother is really the uncrowned
King of Arabia. I wonder what they say to him,
        those odd, uncanny, women,
        my twilight sisters, guarded by unicorns.

My Father

He never looked at anyone, not even me, like once
On one of those official city mornings, he stepped
      right on my foot in the middle of the road
      and kept on walking into nowhere.

He had inherited enough money for him to sail yachts
And shoot pheasants, and ride hard and drink hard
      until she tamed him with her fairy tales
      about God, and how He loved the sinner,
Not the sin. I wonder what he thought of his five
      little bastards. It was impossible to tell.

Now I'm very much like that country gentleman, in that
I can talk to you for hours without for a moment revealing
      that I don't have a clue who you are;
I never look at a man's face and never recognize one;
      I have never been sure of the color of my eyes.

Sometimes he looked so lost that I wanted to show him
The way back home, but the house had become a place
      of thunder; it stared at us with square,
      unseeing eyes, and I never knew why
He went to her in that permanent, resounding dark.

I suppose he might have been a lion of a man, but
When you castrate a lion, all its mane falls out and
            it mews like a cat. Imagine, he was afraid
            of everything; I, of nothing – (my key
            opened all the houses on the street, I thought).

Once as a boy I asked someone if a statue I stared at
Was alive. They said no, but they were wrong. It was.

ANIMAL SPIRITS

Is it true, then, that one fears all that one loves?
These spirits are my awful companions; I can't tell
          anyone when they move in me.
They are so mighty they are unclean; it is the end
Of cleanliness; it is the great crime.

I can only kill them by becoming them. They are all
I have ever loved or wanted; their hooves and paws
          smell of honey and trodden flowers.

Those who do not know me sip their bitter coffee
          and mutter of war. They do not know
          I am wrestling with the spirits
          and have almost won. They do not know
I am looking out from the camels' eyes, out
          from the eyes of the horses.

It is vile to love them; I will not love them.

                              Look –

My brain is sudden and silent as a wildcat.

                              Lord,
Teach me to be lean, and wise. Nothing matters,
          nothing *matters*.

APOLOGIES

I did not choose Arabia; it chose me. The shabby money
That the desert offered us bought lies, bought victory.
                    What was I, that soiled Outsider, doing
Among them? I was not becoming one of them, no matter
What you think. They found it easier to learn my kind
                    of Arabic, than to teach me theirs.
And they were all mad; they mounted their horses and camels
                    from the right.

But my mind's twin kingdoms waged an everlasting war;
The reckless Bedouin and the civilized Englishman
                    fought for control so that I, whatever I was,
Fell into a dumb void that even a false god could not fill,
                    could not inhabit.

The Arabs are children of the idea; dangle an idea
In front of them, and you can swing them wherever.
                    I was also a child of the idea; I wanted
                    no liberty for myself, but to bestow it
Upon them. I wanted to present them with a gift so fine
                    it would outshine all other gifts in their eyes;
                    it would be *worthy*. Then I at last could be
Empty.

You can't imagine how beautiful it is to be empty.
Out of this grand emptiness wonderful things must surely
                    come into being.
When we set out, it was morning. We hardly knew
That when we moved we would not be an army, but a world.

SOLAR WIND

It comes upon you unawares –
                                    something racing out of the edge
Of your vision, as when you are staring at something
            and not staring – looking through –
A herd of white horses grazing on the periphery
Of your sight, and the afternoon
                                    slanting into night –

Comes the wind that is
                        the color of the sun, and your eyes
            which are nuggets of gold follow it
            down the barrels of the rifles, through
            the gun-cotton, and over the culverts,
Leaving everything gold, gold in its wake.

The past and the future are burning up; the present
            melts down the middle, a river of wind,
            wind from the sun, gold wind, anything –
And suddenly you know that all the mysteries have been
solved
            for you, all questions answered.

You must find a god to worship or you will die
In that unholy moment just before darkness and the sound
Of guns.

TAFAS

We came to the village after the Turks. Everyone was
                                          dead,
Except a little girl who came out from the shadows
                                          with
A fibrous hole gaping where her neck and body joined;
                                          she
Cried *don't hit me, Baba*, then hobbled away and fell

Down in a little heap.
                      And then, I think, she died.

Death's little silver cock was struck
                              between her mother's legs;
She sat on the tip of a saw
                      bayonet. And a pregnant woman
Was bent over a sheepfold,
                      the hilt of Hell's sword
Sticking up from where
                      the fetus was, into the air.
                                    And others
Were pinned by legs and arms to the ground like
                                  insects
Mounted by an insane collector.
                          We went after the Turks
And killed them all.
                    Then we blew in the heads of the animals.
The sweet salt blood
                  of the child ran out and out
                                and on and on
All the way to Damascus.
                    All this happened as I have said, and
The next day was Friday.

TALL TALES

It has been said that I sometimes lie, or bend the truth
        to suit me. Did I make that four hundred mile
        trip alone in Turkish territory or not?
        I wonder if it is anybody's business
        to know. Syria is still there,
        and the long lie that the war was.

Was there a poster of me offering money for my capture,
        and did I stand there staring at myself,
        daring anyone to know me? Consider
        truth and untruth, consider why they call them
        the *theatres* of war. All of us
        played our roles to the hilt.

Poets only play with words, you know; they too
        are masters of the Lie, the Grand Fiction.
        Poets and men like me who fight for something
        contained in words, but not words.

What if the whole show was a lie, and it bloody well was –
        would I still lie to you? Of course I would.

There Is No Place To Hide

Here is a famous world; I'm standing on a stage
With ten spotlights on me, talking about how I detest
        publicity. I stand there like an ass,
        apologizing for having a past, a soul,
        a name (which one?), and then
        back shyly into the limelight.

No. What I'm really doing is standing in an unlit room
Holding a court martial upon myself. Shaw tells me
        that to live under a cloud
        is to defame God. I can neither reveal myself
        nor hide. No matter what I do, I am naked.
I can clothe myself in silk or chain mail, and I
        am naked; everything shows through
        and yet no one can see me.

Can you imagine that posterity will call me wonderful
        on the basis of a few pencil sketches,
        a revolt in the desert,
        and my irresistibly foul soul?
Outside my window, a small tit bird bashes itself
        against the glass. At first I thought
        it was admiring itself in the window.
        Now I know it's mad.

Notes From the Dead Land

I have died at last, Feisal. I have been lying
On this hospital bed for five days, and I know
        that I am dead. I was going back home
        on my big bike, and I wasn't doing more
        than sixty when this black van, death camel,
Slid back from the left side of my head, and ahead,
Two boys on little bikes were biking along, and
        something in my head, some brutal music
        played on and on. I was going too fast,
        I was always going too fast for the world,
So I swerved and fell on my stupid head, right
In the middle of the road. I addressed myself
        to the dark hearts of the tall trees
        and nothing answered.

The Arabs say that when you pray, two angels stand
On either side of you, recording good and bad deeds;
        and you should acknowledge them.
        Lying here, I decide that now
        the world can have me any way it pleases.
I will celebrate my perfect death here. *Maktub*:
It is written. I salute both of the angels.

V.

From *Afterworlds*
1987

LATE SONG

When it is all over – the crying and the dancing and the long
                  exhausting music – I will remember only
How once you flirted with your death and lifted your dark
   eyes
                  to warn me of the world's end
As wild leaves fell, and midnight crashed upon the city.

But it is never over; nothing ends until we want it to.
                Look, in shattered midnights,
On black ice under silver trees, we are still dancing, dancing.

Meet me in an hour at the limits of the city.

THE WAH MAI CAFÉ

There's nothing new here; it's just how you pay for it.

Actually *it's* not here anymore, but it was
Near a theatre where Blackstone made everything disappear
And an aging stripper made her tits circle simultaneously
In two opposite directions
And an androgynous angel they called Billy
Appeared at midnight.

So I'd go in my brown corduroy jumper and sit
And take notes because I Was Going To Be A Writer
And when one of the hookers Lily asked me what the hell
I was doing, I said I had to see the seamier side of life,
Etc. She said: You're OK, you can stay.

At the Wah Mai Café Lily would bum cigarettes off me
After she'd turned a trick down the lane
Until the night the cops raided the place and Lily said
Goodbye, Goodbye, as they took some pimps and hookers
away.

Who the hell are you, one cop asked me, gazing in disbelief
At my brown corduroy jumper. I Am a Writer, I said,
And I work at Boys and Girls House which is
A children's library. Actually I'm just a page
But one day I'm going to be a Book.

For Christ's sake go home, said the cop, so I left
And I'm telling you, would I lie to you, it was wonderful
And awful, me and Lily and the others in the Wah Mai Café

All going out into the seamy night in opposite directions,
Some of them disappearing down the lane, me hopping a
streetcar,

All of us trying to find our way back home.

Manitou Poem

'To enter this world was to step into, not out of, the real world.'
– Selwyn Dewdney, *The Sacred Scrolls of the Southern Ojibway*

So I must stand away from the stone to enter the stone,
To dream the idea of the stone, the stone which is all stones,
       the first and final stone,
Its source being, its manitou.

As in puberty I dreamed my lifelong protector, who showed
  me
How to navigate impossible rivers, who made me as the world's
       first person, breathing
Fire and poetry.

The strangers who divided the world into good and evil were
  wrong.
The Great Lynx Misshipeshu who dwells beneath ambivalent
  water
       is both benevolent
Lord, and devil.

And I am become the powerful dreamer who dreams his way
  through
To reality, to enter and ignite the stone, to illumine
       from within
Its perfect paradox, its name.

GREY OWL'S POEM

There is no chart of his movement through the borrowed
        forest,
A place so alien that all he could do with it
                was pretend it was his own
And turn himself into an Indian, savage and lean,
A hunter of the forest's excellent green secret.

For all his movements through the forest were
In search of himself, in search of Archie Belaney,
                a lone predator in London
Telling the very king: *I come in peace, brother.*
(The princess thinking how alien he was, how fine.)

Stranger and stranger to return to the forest
With the beavers all laughing at him, baring
                their crazy orange teeth
And the savage secret – if there ever was one –
Never revealed to him. Stranger and stranger to return to

The female forest, the fickle wind erasing his tracks,
The receding treeline, and the snowbanks moving and moving.

THE NAMES

We want to pretend that you are our ancestors –
        you who are called
Wolf in the Water, Blue Flash of Lightning, Heaven Fire,
        Black Sleep –

You who have no devil, no opposite of Manitou.

You who are hiding behind your names, behind
        closed doors of thunder
And will not let us in.

Backlit by blue lightning, the silhouette of the wolf
        drinks the midnight river; fire from heaven
Falls on our sleep and invents morning; the air is thick
        with feathers from surreal birds.

You who never knew the evil in us, you who have
        no opposite of Manitou,
Come out from behind the thunder and embrace us –
All we long to become, all we have never known of ourselves.

Before you are gone from our eyes forever –
        (you who are certainly not our ancestors)
Teach us our names, the names of our cities.

No one ever welcomed us when we came to this land.

FIREWORKS

In memory of Marian Engel

A year after your death, in the spleen of winter
Part of your garden lies buried in my garden
Where I transplanted it. I wonder
Where you are now – (it isn't exactly heaven
because you said once you knew all about heaven
and didn't want to go there). Nevertheless
As I celebrate your life I celebrate your entry
Into some unconditional kingdom.

Friend, let your death be fireworks
Like the pinwheels and burning schoolhouses
(we have so much to unlearn)
You had in your garden on the 24th of May
A hundred years ago when we were less than young.

Let it be a conflagration, a sign,
Like all those loud outspoken flowers
Which will burn all summer in my back yard –
(the Japanese lanterns, bright audacious orange
against the garden wall) –

Everything struggling to become what it already is
And we who are left behind you
Struggling to become what we already are.

Winter 1986

MORNING IN THE BURNED HOUSE

Margaret Atwood

'Margaret Atwood is the quiet Mata Hari, the mysterious, violent figure . . . who pits herself against the ordered, too-clean world like an arsonist' – **Michael Ondaatje**

Margaret Atwood's first new book of poems for over a decade is cause for celebration. By turns dark, playful, intensely moving, tender and intimate – these poems are Atwood's most mature, 'setting foot on the middle ground / between body and word'. Here is that wickedly dry, humorous voice – and here too are personal poems that concern themselves with love, with memory, with the fragility of the natural world. A beautiful elegiac series of meditations on the death of a parent completes this generous and disturbing collection of poems.

☐	Morning in the Burned House	Margaret Atwood	£8.99
☐	Sunris	Grace Nichols	£7.99
☐	Lazy Thoughts of a Lazy Woman	Grace Nichols	£5.99
☐	Rotten Pomerack	Merle Collins	£8.99
☐	We, the Dangerous	Janice Mirikitani	£8.99
☐	Me Again	Stevie Smith	£7.50

Virago now offers an exciting range of quality titles by both established and new authors. All of the books in this series are available from:

Little, Brown and Company (UK),
P.O. Box 11,
Falmouth,
Cornwall TR10 9EN.

Fax No: 01326 317444
Telephone No: 01326 317200
E-mail: books@barni.avel.co.uk

Payments can be made as follows: cheque, postal order (payable to Little, Brown and Company) or by credit cards, Visa/Access. Do not send cash or currency. UK customers and B.F.P.O. please allow £1.00 for postage and packing for the first book, plus 50p for the second book, plus 30p for each additional book up to a maximum charge of £3.00 (7 books plus).

Overseas customers including Ireland, please allow £2.00 for the first book plus £1.00 for the second book, plus 50p for each additional book.

NAME (Block Letters) ....

....

ADDRESS ....

....

....

☐ I enclose my remittance for ....

☐ I wish to pay by Access/Visa Card

Number ⬚⬚⬚⬚⬚⬚⬚⬚⬚⬚⬚⬚⬚⬚⬚⬚

Card Expiry Date ⬚⬚⬚⬚